Fruit and Vegetable Gardening

FRUIT AND VEGETABLE GARDENING

Ethne Clarke

WITH A FOREWORD BY
MAX DAVIDSON

SUNBURST BOOKS

This edition first published in 1995 by
Sunburst Books,
Deacon House,
65 Old Church Street,
London SW3 5BS.

ISBN 1 85778 167 8

Publishing Manager *Casey Horton*
Editor *Paul Brewer*
Designer *Ming Cheung*

Publisher's Note
Readers should note that plant breeders introduce new cultivars all the time.
Please check your seed catalogues for the latest ones.

> **WARNING**
> If using chemical
> herbicides, fungicides or insecticides,
> be sure to follow exactly
> the manufacturer's instructions.

Printed and bound in Hong Kong

CONTENTS

FOREWORD

Growing one's own fruit and vegetables in the garden is probably the closest most of us will ever get to being sturdy independent farmers like our ancestors. In an age when society tries to impose a bland conformity on us, here is an alternative to supermarket produce.

The aspiring gardener examining their plot may consider it far too small for planting fruits and vegetables. But advances in horticulture have come to the rescue. Changes to the way apples and pears are cultivated, for instance, make possible a mini orchard in the garden. The secret is to have bush apple trees grown on M27 rootstocks which are unlikely ever to be more than 1.8m/6 ft tall, and to buy pear trees, trained in two-tier espalier form, to plant along a low boundary fence.

The modern farmer seeks high-yielding apples to get a good return on the investment of time and money in tending an orchard. However, the part-time gardener can take taste and variety into consideration. Old-fashioned varieties with virtues almost forgotten such as 'Egremont Russet', 'Worcester Pearmain' and 'Orleans Reinette' will make a welcome change from the more familiar 'Golden Delicious', 'Cox's' or 'Granny Smith'.

Fruit that supermarkets provide from Mediterranean countries can be grown here, and you can prove it by doing just that. The popular apricot 'Moorpark' has been grown successfully in England since 1760, and 'Peregrine' and 'Rochester' peaches from the garden, with their unexpectedly large size and juicy flavour, have delighted several generations of Britons.

Growing our own vegetables likewise enables us to have a better choice of varieties. It need never be limited to those roots and greens which we feel we ought to have. The sweetest little tomatoes come from varieties such as 'Gardener's Delight' and 'Tumbler'. We can grow perfect courgettes as well as pumpkins and squash.

'New' can mean an improvement for the good. Using the compact canes of 'Loch Ness' or 'Waldo', the owner of even the tiniest of gardens can grow blackberries. There is less need to spray raspberries bred to be resistant to greenfly and disease. With 'Glen Prosen', 'Glen Moy' or 'Glen Garry', success is virtually assured.

Techniques for vegetables have changed too. Gone are the old-fashioned raised asparagus beds. Nowadays we can grow asparagus much like any other vegetable. Similarly celery is rarely grown in trenches. Most gardeners now prefer the much easier to cultivate self-blanching kind.

One welcome development from the *nouvelle cuisine* has been the introduction of baby vegetables and the breeding of new varieties for the close-growing type of cultivation. This is marvellous news for all gardeners who may have believed that you needed an allotment to have a wide range of produce. With cauliflowers the size of tennis balls grown at a 12.5 cm/5 in spacing and savoy cabbages just large enough to provide a meal for two spaced a mere 10 cm/4 in apart in the vegetable plot, all sorts of things become possible.

Medical experts tell us that for a healthier diet we need to eat more fresh fruit and vegetables. And what could be fresher than an apple just picked from the tree or some carrots just pulled from the ground in your own garden?

MAX DAVIDSON

INTRODUCTION

For many people, the idea of growing their own fruit and vegetables is firmly linked to the notion of self-sufficiency. I have to admit to a sneaking envy for those gardeners so organised that crops are sown in regular succession, whose carrots and parsnips are harvested and perfectly stored, whose onions never rot and whose lettuces never bolt. They can manage to raise exactly the right amount of courgettes and tomatoes and so never have to try to dispose of sad little bundles of unwanted veg on neighbours who usually have grown too much themselves. They are a model for us all, but I am not one of them.

I have grown vegetables ever since I could plant a seed. My earliest efforts, during a childhood in the Midwestern United States, were with sweet corn. It grew well. The plants were quite spectacular, towering over me like a crowd of giants. But best of all, the ears of corn, cooked within minutes of picking, tasted as sweet as honey. My next success was with pumpkins I wanted for Hallowe'en, and I grew some whoppers. Then came tomatoes. Sun-warmed, straight from the vine, the flavour was ambrosial.

My mature gardening efforts (which never quite match up to the memory of my childhood triumphs) have been in London and Norfolk, and in both places the first task was to create a kitchen garden. In the former I acquired an allotment – which I never successfully tamed. In Norfolk, where I have made a garden from 6000 sq m/1.5 acres of paddock, the kitchen garden was made almost before the moving van had departed – among the packing crates were several 'heritage' varieties of potato growing in well-rotted compost. It was deliberately sited close to the house; the allotment had been a car-journey away, this garden was on the doorstep.

I still grow the same vegetables as I enjoyed in my childhood, but each year I add a few oddities gathered on travels abroad. Joy Larkcom, who has written several brilliant books about vegetable growing, has also been a great inspiration. She has introduced many delicious Oriental vegetables and salad herbs to seed suppliers and thus to our gardens, and grows beautiful edible flowers and herbs among the unfamiliar veg and fruit with which she is constantly experimenting.

That is what my vegetable and fruit garden is for: growing the varieties and produce I can't find in the market. Commercial varieties are bred for durability – some of the produce has travelled thousands of miles before arriving on supermarket shelves – and long shelf-life. In these circumstances, flavour and quality are bound to suffer. I can buy anything I grow, but I'd rather harvest little yellow 'Sungold' tomatoes than buy a pound of 'Alicante'. Sweet corn may be several days old by the time you put it in your shopping trolley, and in the those days its sugar content will have turned to tasteless starch. 'Golden Delicious' are pleasantly crunchy, but nothing equals the succulent sweetness of the old apple varieties; it is notoriously difficult to purchase a pear that it isn't either bullet hard or cotton-wool mushy, but if you pick your own the flavour and texture are nearly always perfect.

Variety, profit, personal satisfaction, health and well-being are all reasons for growing your own fruit and vegetables – but it is also a lot of fun.

THE FRUIT AND VEGETABLE GARDEN

IF YOU ARE A BEGINNER AT GARDENING, growing fruit and vegetables is probably the best place to start. All the skills of gardening are employed in the kitchen garden: seed sowing, digging, weeding, planting, fertilising, and so on. It will also teach you some of gardening's finer points, such as soil pH, types of plant nutrient, and even a lesson or two about botany. In addition to gaining knowledge of one of life's most pleasurable pastimes – gardening – you will derive enormous pleasure from providing food for your table that is as fresh as the moment it was picked. Believe me, there is nothing nicer than crisp lettuces, sweet carrots and sun-ripened tomatoes from your own patch. Are you convinced? Then let us begin.

Where Will Your Garden Grow?

First you must consider where to place your vegetable garden. If you are going to cultivate an allotment, this decision will be out of your hands. But if it's to be in your private garden, try to put the plot near a source of water, and not too far from the kitchen door. Vegetables are pretty plants with a wide variety of foliage shapes and textures, flowers and fruit, so don't feel the patch has to be tucked away behind the shed or screened by trellis, those are options not rules.

The plot should be located in a spot that receives maximum sunshine and where it will not be exposed to high winds; in fact the more shelter from wind you can provide for the vegetable garden, the better your harvest will be.

Compost is the other factor that plays an important role in high yields. It acts as a soil conditioner, helps to retain moisture in the soil, introduces beneficial organisms to the soil and generally helps in every aspect of gardening. Anything that will rot can be made into compost. The only exceptions are meat and bones (they attract vermin), perennial weed roots (they will survive) and diseased plant material, which should be burned

ABOVE: **A traditional-style cottage garden mingles flowers and vegetables.**

RIGHT: **These runner bean plants, grown on a tepee made from bamboo canes, add a structural element to the kitchen garden.**

(put the ashes on the heap by all means). Leaves should be given their own heap since they are slower to rot and are best used for mulch.

'Heap' is a misleading name, making the composting material sound like a pile of rubbish. There is more to it than that. In my garden, the compost heap is actually two 'bins' made from four pieces of corrugated tin sheeting, nailed to supporting posts to form a letter *E*. I fill one bin, then turn it over into its empty neighbour, and then begin again. By the time that bin is full, the first is ready to be dug into the garden, its space filled with the turned heap, and a fresh one started.

ABOVE: A traditional kitchen garden layout of four squares divided by narrow paths. Such a plan aids crop rotation.

ABOVE: A well-planned vegetable garden is a handsome sight. Brassicas are grown with French marigolds, which can deter a number of insect pests.

All material destined for the compost should be broken up before adding it to the heap. Some people run their kitchen waste through the food processor, others spread it on the ground and run the lawn mower over it catching the chopped up refuse in the clipping box – not a very tidy operation! Those are refinements that will speed the process of decomposition, but it is enough to crush the egg shells and break up really thick stalks. The best way to prepare garden waste for composting is to invest in a shredder. These come in various sizes and for most domestic gardens an electric model is adequate. My garden is one-and-a-half acres and I use an Al-Ko H 1600 to clear all the garden waste; it shreds green sappy branches up to 3 cm/1⅛ in diameter, so there is no need for bonfires or trips to the council rubbish dump. The smaller your garden, the less powerful a shredder you'll need.

If you haven't got the space available in your garden for a fixed compost heap, there are purpose-made composting containers that you can buy from most garden centres.

How Will Your Garden Grow?

If this is your first attempt at vegetables, don't be overambitious and dig up the whole garden. Begin in small steps; decide what you want to grow and how much. I wouldn't advise aiming at self-sufficiency in the first year. Grow the things you can't buy in the market; select unusual varieties such as red lettuce or yellow courgettes; potatoes take up a lot of space, but there should be room for a row of first early potatoes. Do grow some herbs and a tomato plant or two. By concentrating on doing a few things well, your early rewards will be all the sweeter, and encourage you to greater feats of gardening in the coming years.

Whether you are gardening in an allotment or beginning in the back garden, you must clear the ground first. The easiest way to do this is to spray with a glyphosate herbicide such as Round-Up. This is translocating weed killer, which means that the poison is taken into the root system through the leaves, killing top growth and roots. Most uncultivated ground and lawns will have some perennial weed roots, and although these can be removed when digging, it is difficult to be thorough; it's no joke that one little crumb of couch grass root left in the soil will soon develop into a strapping network of strangling roots. Spraying off the entire plant allows you to dig in all the dead turf and weeds, which is not that different to digging in manure or compost.

Digging over the garden need not be the back-breaking chore you imagine if you approach it methodically. Don't try to do the whole job in one day. Most back injuries happen to gardeners who charge out on the first fine day and attempt to complete all the heavy tasks immediately. Use a clean spade and fork – stainless steel to make the job easier since soil slides off this surface. Measure out your plot, marking the perimeter with stakes and string to keep edges straight. Begin the digging at one end, working your way across the plot, rather than down its length.

Dump a barrowful of compost or well-rotted manure at the end where you will begin. Remove the first trench of soil, putting it in the barrow, then wheel it down to where you will finish.

Unless your soil is very heavy there should be no need to double dig. This means removing the soil to a level of more than two spade-depths to break up the topsoil. You will have to do this if the soil drains poorly, but be sure to keep the subsoil you remove separate from the topsoil. Incorporate rubble, gravel and compost into the bottom of the double-dug trench and then return the topsoil. However, on a single-dug plot, simply add the compost to the bottom of the trench. Then, as you dig the next trench, turn the soil from it over into the previously dug trench. When you reach the end of the plot, the soil removed from the first trench will be there waiting for you.

ABOVE: A floating mulch of horticultural fleece protects these early potatoes from spring frosts.

RIGHT: Potatoes are an excellent choice for the first crop on previously uncropped soil because they require so much digging.

Seed Sowing

Seed can be sown in trays to germinate indoors in warmth. It can also be sown in 'cell-trays' to produce individual plants, or in pots to prick out after the first true leaves have formed. The plants are then raised in the greenhouse or on the windowsill until it is warm enough to plant them out. This is discussed in more detail on page 16.

Usually, seed is sown directly into the garden. Do this on a still day, when the soil is moist and there is a chance of rain. To sow the seed in rows, use a garden line to mark out a straight line across the bed. A piece of string attached to two sticks will suffice, although spike-and-reel assemblies can be bought. Keep the line on the ground, not above it. Take the garden rake and use one corner of it to draw out a shallow trench along the marked line. Water the trench lightly. Sow the seed as required and then use the rake to pull the soil gently back over the row. Water again using a fine spray.

BELOW: Grow a late calabrese broccoli, such as 'Romanesco', for a taste of a vegetable less commonly found on supermarket shelves.

Most seed is sown in early summer after the soil has warmed up. Earlier sowings can, however, be made by using cloches to cover the soil in late February-early March. There are many different sorts of cloche available made of either glass or plastic, which is the least expensive. Simply put the cloche over the place where you intend to make early sowings, holding the edges of plastic cloches in place with stones or soil. A cloche captures the sun's warmth and in a few weeks you can begin sowing.

LEFT: The 'Milan White' turnip is a brassica, but a root crop too.

LEFT: The 'Milan White' turnip is a brassica, but a root crop too.

ABOVE: Celery is a salad legume. This 'American Green' variety is self-blanching.

Crop Rotation

Vegetables divide into three groups; legumes (peas and beans), including salads, other leafy crops and members of the onion family; brassicas, which includes all members of the cabbage family (Brussels sprouts, cauliflower, broccoli, and also turnips, swedes and radishes); and roots (potatoes, carrots, parsnips, beetroot and so on).

Each group should be grown in a different part of the garden each year. Growing them in the same spot over several consecutive years will deplete the soil of the nutrients each requires for healthy growth.

Legumes and salads require freshly manured soil that is high in nitrogen; roots do best in the previous year's manured soil to which a general purpose fertiliser has been added; brassicas like soil that has been dressed with a general-purpose fertiliser, but are not that keen on manure. They also like a slightly alkaline soil, so be sure to give them a light dusting of garden lime.

You should rotate your crops in the following order: first legumes, then root crops, followed by brassicas, then back to legumes. If you keep a garden plan with the location of each group updated every year, you will have a clear idea of what point you are at in the rotation system.

BELOW: Brussels sprouts are a leafy brassica.

RIGHT: Here lettuce and beans are grown together. The contrast of their leaf shape and the form of each vegetable makes an attractive feature in the garden.

What Should Your Garden Grow?

With the seed catalogues spread out before you in winter, or when studying the seed displays in garden centres, it is easy to be confounded. There is a huge choice, but there are a few guides to help you. Many of the seeds are for old varieties, trusted and true. But these may not have the disease-resistant qualities of new varieties that have benefited from the advances in horticultural technology, and been bred to withstand the pests and diseases commonly associated with certain vegetables. F_1 hybrids will produce uniform crops of high-quality vegetables, achieved by cross-breeding varieties selected for these characteristics; F_1 seed tends to be more expensive that standard vegetable seed varieties. The Royal Horticultural Society tests many vegetables and awards them marks of quality: the highest award is FCC (First Class Certificate), followed by AM (Award of Merit) and HC (Highly Commended). These awards are a good indication of garden worthiness.

Some seed will be pelleted, meaning that the individual seed is embedded in a protective coating, creating a little round ball that is easy to station sow. Other seed may be dressed or treated to enhance its disease resistance – like giving it a vaccination before sowing.

BELOW: You can even fit your fruit garden in a window box. These are strawberries.

It is also possible to buy ready-rooted seedlings of some varieties, and while this can save time or allow you to fill a gap quickly, it's cheaper to grow your own seedlings in a tray for transplanting.

Some vegetables, such as tomatoes, benefit from being sown early 'under glass'. In other words in a seed tray indoors, where the warmth will help them to germinate quickly so that they have already grown into substantial plants when planted out.

The easiest way to do this is to fill a pot with moist seed compost, scatter the seed thinly and evenly over the surface of the soil and sieve a fine layer of compost over the seed. Water gently and put the pot into a plastic bag. Seal the bag with a wire twist and put the pot in a warm dark place, such as an airing cupboard – but not over the direct heat of radiator or boiler – and the seed should germinate in a week to 10 days. As soon as you see the seed is beginning to germinate, and is pushing through the soil, move the pot into the light.

When the seedlings are large enough to be handled, which will be when the first true leaves (as opposed to the seed leaves) develop, lift them gently from the compost using the end of a pencil or other small tool. Never hold the seedling by the stem! Always hold it by one of the leaves; if the leaf breaks it will be replaced by another, but there is no way to repair a damaged stem.

Prick out the individual seedlings of such large vegetable plants as corn and tomatoes into separate pots; lettuces and herbs can be pricked out in rows in trays. Don't crowd them, though; they need room to develop into strong plants and if planted less than about 2.5 cm/1 in apart will become weak and straggly as they fight each other for food and light. In a standard seed tray, about five plants across and six down (30 plants) is a good average.

'Damping off' is a problem that affects transplanted seedlings; the botrytis virus attacks the stem at soil level and the plantlet shrivels. To prevent this happening, add a fungicide such as Benlate to the water before watering the trays or pots prior to pricking out. Put the trays in a warm sunny place for the plants to grow on. Several weeks before planting out, begin to 'harden off' the plantlets by moving them outdoors. Do not, however, leave them out overnight until you are quite sure that all danger of frost is past.

Large seeds for beans and peas can also be started under glass. Sow individual seeds into separate pots, or into the special cell or plug trays that are now widely available.

ABOVE: Lilies and strawberries grown in the same container.

RIGHT: This gardener has put tomatoes, lettuces, carrots and parsley in with marigolds and nasturtiums.

Seed can also be sown outdoors into 'seedbeds'. This is the usual way to start leeks, cabbages, mid-season lettuces and a few other vegetables that do not mind being transplanted. A seedbed is nothing more than a section of the vegetable garden where the soil has been raked down to fine tilth, with no large stones or obstructions to get in the way of tiny developing seedlings. I like to add extra grit to the seedbed soil to be sure it is quite 'open', thus making it easy for strong root systems to develop. Seed is sown into shallow drills as described above, and you can begin thinning once the seedlings develop their first true leaves. This serves the same purpose as pricking out into trays, and involves carefully removing some of the seedlings, trying to leave individual plants spaced equally along the row. From there they can be transplanted to their growing place and be left to mature.

Thinning is also practised on crops sown *in situ* (the place where they will grow and mature); thinnings from plots of leafy vegetables can be used to make salads.

When transplanting from seedbeds to rows, water the plantlets well a few hours before you plan to lift them. It is best to do the job in late afternoon on a still, overcast day. Use the tip of your trowel to make a planting hole large enough to take the root ball of the plant. Hold the plant by the leaves and drop it into place. Firm the soil around the base of the plant to make sure it gets a good hold, and water in.

ABOVE: **Swiss chard and radicchio in a winter pot.**

ABOVE: **These artichoke plants are ready to be pricked out.**

RIGHT: **Peas are best when cooked minutes after picking.**

LEFT: **A rabbit has made a meal of these leeks.**

Pests and Diseases

The best way to have healthy crops is to give them healthy growing conditions; poorly drained soil, plots overrun with weeds, or where no attention has been paid to crop rotation will be a haven for every bug or virus that comes along.

Raise your plants in good conditions, transplant only the healthiest seedlings, keep the plot free of garden debris (fallen leaves, faded vegetables, pulled weeds and so on).

TACKLING PROBLEMS

Aphids, caterpillars, carrot fly, flea beetles, and cabbage-root fly are the main enemies of the vegetable gardener. But there is an arsenal of sprays and powders to help win the battle.

Direct sprays that kill insects on contact are on the whole cheap, and often made using the roots or flowers of other plants, which means they are marginally safer and less damaging to the environment. These include derris and pyrethrum available as powder or liquid.

Systemic insecticides are chemical-based poisons, and must be used with caution in order not to do lasting damage to yourself or the envi-

ABOVE: **Too much watering can cause tomatoes problems.**

ronment. Their lethal effect is achieved by being absorbed into the body of the pest that feeds on the plant that has been sprayed. Always spray on a windless day to keep the poison from drifting on other plants, and do so on an overcast day in the early evening – beneficial flying insects such as bees are no longer flying then. Biocontrols are chemical free, consisting of bacteria spores that are completely safe to everything except caterpillars. Spray *Bascillus thuringiensis* var. *kurstaki* on brassicas to prevent any infestation by cabbage moth.

ABOVE: Blackfly have got at these beans.

ABOVE RIGHT: A scarecrow can be a decorative feature as well.

Slugs and snails will be a problem in heavy, wet ground. There are slug poisons in pellet, liquid or gel form, but they must be used with care to avoid poisoning family and pets. It's a good idea to cover the scattered pellets with the rind of half a grapefruit or an overturned flowerpot. Club root is a soil-borne disease affecting brassicas. The roots of young plants should be dipped into calomel powder before planting. If late summer is particularly wet, potatoes and tomatoes can be damaged by blight, appearing as brown patches on leaves and fruit. Spray with a copper-based fungicide such as Bordeaux mixture in midsummer. Virus diseases of cucumbers, marrows and melons cause the foliage and stems to become distorted and stunt the growth of developing fruit. The only thing to do is dig up the plant and burn it.

THE VEGETABLES

The vegetable gardener puts in a lot of work to secure a crop. But the rewards, better flavour and more control over varieties sown, can make all that effort worthwhile.

Salad crops

LETTUCES

Lettuces can be grown in full sun or dappled shade and require a moist soil and open position to avoid the possibility of mildew. They should be grown on soil that has been freshly manured. Sow the seed *in situ* or – for early crops – sow it under glass and prick out to have individual plants for setting out later.

Water the ground well before sowing. Lettuce germinates better if it is sown in the cool of the evening rather than the heat of the day. Choose a still, moist evening for the job.

There are dozens of lettuces to choose from, and any good seed catalogue will provide you with plenty of ideas. Among my favourites is 'Tom Thumb', which makes small, tightly packed cos-type lettuces early in the year. Loose-leaf lettuces are good for 'cut-and-come-again'; in other words, cut just as many leaves as you need from each plant. Fresh leaves will grow again. The serrated leaves of the 'Salad Bowl' are shaped like an oak leaf (there is a red-leafed form), and 'Lollo Biondi' and 'Lollo Rossa' are bright green and red varieties of an exceptionally frilly lettuce. 'All the Year Round' is good for early sowing under cloches, and 'Winter Density' is a cos-type lettuce that can be autumn sown for 'overwintering', or growing on under cloche protection.

Other salad leaves to grow include rocket – also known as arugula – which has a peppery, almost meaty flavour; a few leaves will spark up a bowl of plain greenery. American or land cress also has a hot tang. These can be broadcast sown in a small patch from spring and through summer, while seed sown in the autumn will produce greenery for early spring.

ABOVE: Butterhead and loose leaf lettuces growing together.

RIGHT: A cloche will extend the lettuce growing season.

22

Spinach is not everyone's favourite, but there are few vegetables so rich in vitamins and minerals. Summer spinach varieties such as 'Bloomsdale' have smooth seeds and can be sown from the end of winter throughout summer in partly shaded, rich, moist soil. Winter spinach such as 'Prickly Winter' has knobbly seeds (hence the name) and should be sown during the autumn to crop the following spring. Make the rows for each about 30 cm/12 in apart and thin to 15 cm/6 in between plants. Use the tender thinnings for salads.

Radishes are among the easiest vegetables to grow; a sprinkle of seed every other week from early spring to summer's end will provide a steady crop of crunchy, ruby-tinted roots that add savour to salads and sandwiches. Sow the seed in rows about 15 cm/6 in apart, or in between rows of slower-maturing vegetables. Take time to thin the seedlings to about 2 cm/1 in apart as crowded plants go straight to seed. Radishes, rocket and American cress all suffer from flea beetle, but a dusting of derris keeps the crop clean.

Ridge cucumbers are also easy to grow, and F_1 hybrids are as smooth-skinned and sweet as glasshouse varieties. There are bush sorts which can be raised in containers as well as the open garden, and trailing sorts to grow up supports or on the ground using a straw mulch to keep the fruit clean. The soil for cucumbers should be rich and deeply dug, with plenty of water during the growing season. The seed is large so can be station sown into holes about 30 cm/12 in apart into which compost or manure has been dug before planting.

Sow spring onions such as 'White Lisbon' and 'Paris Silverskin' in shallow drills in rows about 10 cm/4 in apart. Do not thin the seedlings; let them grow and pull as needed.

It is possible to grow tomatoes outdoors, but the further north your garden is, the sunnier the spot you plant them will have to be. Start the seed indoors in trays or individual pots in early spring and prick out seedlings or thin pot sowings as soon as the first true leaves have developed. Keep the developing plants well watered and plant out as soon as all danger of frosts has passed.

Plant them in rows about 15 cm/18 in apart with 60 cm/2 ft between the rows. Plant them deeply, burying the stem up to the first pair of leaves; feeding roots will develop along the buried stem, allowing the

ABOVE: Spinach is highly nutritious and tasty if cooked properly, but has a tendency to bolt in warm weather.

plant to take up plenty of water and nutrients. Tie the main stems to sturdy bamboo canes as they grow, and pinch out the side shoots that develop in the leaf axils (where the leaf meets the stem). When there are about 5 fruit trusses, pinch out the tip of the main stem to stop growth. As the fruit develops, water regularly to avoid blossom end rot and splitting skins.

'Ailsa Craig' is an old favourite, but I like to grow 'San Marzano', an Italian plum tomato that is good eating whether fresh or cooked.

Roots and Tubers

I wouldn't be the first gardener who has weeded out a row of parsnips! I like to mix the parsnip seed with radish seed that germinates quickly, opening the soil, and also marking the row where the parsnips are yet to appear. Sow the seed *in situ* in rows about 30 cm/12 in apart. Once the seedlings are large enough to handle easily, thin to about 10 cm/4 in between plants for small roots, 15 cm/6 in for larger ones. Parsnips are ready to harvest from mid to late October, although some gardeners always wait for the first frost, which they claim improves the taste. Lift the roots as required. 'Avonresister' is a good all-purpose variety with resistance to canker (a scabby disfiguration of the skin).

Carrot seed for early crops can be sown under cloches in early spring while main-crop carrots should be sown when the soil has begun to warm.

BELOW: **The slow-growing parsnip requires little attention.**

Plant them in rows about 15 cm/6 in apart, and thin out the seedlings to about 8 cm/3 in apart; do this gradually, pulling the largest seedlings each time and leaving the less mature to develop. Water the row well before thinning, and work in the evening to lessen the moisture loss from the disturbed rows. Use the tiny carrots in salads or as baby cooked vegetables.

Carrot fly is the main pest, but sowing onions nearby can help disguise the scent of the carrots, which is how the fly finds its quarry. In this respect, it also helps to clear the thinnings from the row and firm the soil back around the remaining plants. The variety 'Sytan' is bred to resist carrot fly and there are other varieties engineered to lack the scent-producing chemical that attracts carrot fly. Other varieties worth growing are 'Early Nantes' and 'Rondo', which makes stumpy, almost round roots.

Freshly picked beetroot, pulled when the size of a golfball, steamed and served with lashings of melted butter and black pepper are one of the rewards of vegetable gardening. Sow the seed in late spring; it is large enough to station sow, about every 8 cm/3 in in rows 15 cm/6 in apart. Make successional sowings throughout the summer. Beetroot can also be sown between the rows of other crops. 'Boltardy' is a popular variety since it is slow to run to seed; 'Detroit' is an old favourite; 'Golden' is a yellow-fleshed variety; and 'Little Ball' is just that, making tiny roots that are ideally suited to pickling whole.

Unless you have plenty of space and are willing to write off part of it indefinitely, I would not recommend growing Jerusalem artichoke. Once you've planted it, it's there for life; even the most dedicated digging will not banish it from the ground. And it creeps about. However, some people enjoy the earthy taste and it is another member of the limited winter vegetable community.

The plants grow to 3m/10 ft or more from tubers that should be planted in early spring, but the top growth should be cut down by half in midsummer to help the plants produce large tubers. The roots can be harvested during winter as needed.

All these root crops like a light, well-drained soil.

ABOVE: Carrots were originally grown for their frilly leaves, which were worn by 17th-century fashion victims. We grow them for their vitamin-rich roots.

BELOW: Globe-shaped beetroot matures quickly and is delicious hot or in salads.

ABOVE: **The Jerusalem artichoke is harvested in winter.**

ABOVE: **It is a good idea to thin your carrots. The baby ones can be cooked or used in salads.**

Potatoes are divided into three main groups according to cropping order: *first earlies*, planted from early spring and lifted from early summer; plant *second earlies* in mid-spring, these take longer to reach maturity and can be lifted as needed or left in the ground to mature for storing; and *main crop*, planted in late spring and lifted in late summer once the leafy top growth has withered.

Purchase seed potatoes in late winter and put them to *chit* in trays in a cool place out of direct sunlight. The tubers will begin to make stubby green sprouts from the small eyes dotting the surface. When these shoots are about 2.5 cm/1 in long, the tubers are ready to plant.

They should be placed into individual holes that are between 10-15 cm/4-6 in deep, or in trenches of similar depth. Plant the tubers 25-35 cm/10-15 in apart in rows up to 60 cm/2 ft apart. When the plants are about 20 cm/9 in tall, draw the earth up into mounds over them to be sure that the developing tubers cannot push through the soil; tubers exposed to sunlight become green; this greening is toxic, so the potatoes should not be eaten.

During the growing season, give the plants a liquid feed high in nitrogen, and water regularly – particularly during dry spells. Main crops are especially sensitive to watering. When the tubers are about the size of a marble, the plants should be given a heavy, liberal watering to ensure a good yield.

Spray the plants with a copper-based fungicide to prevent attacks of potato blight.

There are many varieties to choose from. Some, such as 'Pentland Javelin' and 'Maris Piper' are resistant to the eelworm (a soil-borne pest), while others, such as 'Pink Fir Apple', have a waxy flesh that is good for salads. 'Orkney Black' is one of the more unusual varieties, with its inky blue flesh. This fades when cooked to a dirty white, but the flavour is remarkably nutty and sweet. It is possible to get seed potatoes of the varieties you can commonly obtain from greengrocers, but why bother? Take this opportunity to grow something different.

Brassicas

Cabbages can be harvested all year round if you grow a selection from the seasonal groups: winter, spring, summer and autumn harvesting. Within each group there are pointed and ball-head types referring to the shape of the cabbage. There are also red-leafed cabbages.

All cabbages like a firm soil, so prepare the ground well in the autumn, digging in manure or compost. Dust the ground with lime prior to planting, rake the surface just to level it and then tread it down lightly. After you have set out the plants, tread along each row to make sure the roots are firmly in contact with the soil.

Seed should be sown in a nursery bed in rows 15 cm/6 in apart, and then thinned so plantlets are spaced about 8 cm/4 in apart. They are ready to transplant when they have developed five or six leaves; transplanted distances are about 45 cm/18 in apart all round. Sowing timetable and good varieties for seasonal groups are:

Winter cabbages: Sow these during mid to late spring so that they can be transplanted in midsummer. 'Christmas Drumhead' is a small ball-head type, that should be harvested in the autumn; 'Celtic' is an F$_1$ hybrid that makes large heads to harvest from late autumn onwards. Savoy cabbages such as 'Ormskirk' are especially hardy winter cabbages with characteristic deeply crinkled dark green leaves.

Spring cabbage: Sow mid to late summer to transplant at the beginning or in the middle of autumn. 'Pixie' makes small pointed heads with crunchy hearts and is suitable for small gardens. 'Offenham' matures in the

ABOVE: Red cabbages are harvested in the autumn. With careful planning, no vegetable gardener need be without some variety of cabbage.

spring. Its loose-hearted leafy heads can be cut for spring greens.

Summer and autumn cabbage: Sow in late winter under glass or on a seedbed in spring. Transplant in late spring. 'Hispi' grows quickly: if you sow them under glass in late winter, you'll be able to start cutting in summer. 'Primo' makes firm medium-sized ball-heads ideal for for using in coleslaw.

Red cabbage is raised as summer-autumn varieties. F_1 'Ruby Ball' crops early, and is ready for cutting from midsummer onwards.

Like cabbages, Brussels sprouts should be sown in a nursery bed in late winter or early spring for transplanting two or three months later. Set the plants about 60 cm/2 ft apart all round. In late summer give the plants a high nitrogen feed, watering it in thoroughly.

By having plants of several varieties you can harvest from early autumn on into early spring. 'Peer Gynt' crops during the autumn months and into early winter; 'Predora' is ready in mid autumn; 'Fortress' from mid winter to early spring. Gather the buttons from the bottom of the stalk upwards, and be sure to remove any yellowing leaves.

Sprouting broccoli is an easy-to-grow, prolific winter vegetable, and you can cut just as much as you need for a meal. Sow the seed in the spring, transplant to 60 cm/2 ft apart in summer and begin harvesting in late winter. 'Nine Star Perennial' is a purple sprouting sort; 'Early White Sprouting' is just that, making pale yellow florets. Cut the plants regularly to ensure a steady supply of tender young growth.

RIGHT: Cauliflowers need a lot of care to grow successfully, and as a result are generally regarded as the best test of a vegetable gardener's skill.

Cauliflowers are a demanding vegetable, and require as close to perfect conditions as you can provide. So lime the soil (especially if your soil is acid), since they like alkaline conditions; dig in plenty of manure or compost and cultivate the soil deeply. Sow the seed in individual pots so that the roots receive the minimum disturbance when transplanting. Keep the growing plants well supplied with water.

As with cabbages, cauliflowers are seasonal. Varieties for harvesting in summer and autumn, such as 'Dominant' and 'All the Year Round', should be sown in mid autumn, and planted out in early spring for harvesting in early summer. Later crops can be had by sowing in early spring to plant out in late spring and harvest in late summer.

Autumn-to-winter varieties such as 'Snowcap' can be sown in spring for cutting in the autumn.

Winter hardy cauliflowers such as 'St Agnes' are really only suitable for areas with mild winters providing a long growing season and rare frosts. The seed is sown in spring, plants are set out in midsummer and the harvest is from early to late winter. 'Armado April' and 'Maystar' are spring cauliflowers; sow the seed in spring, plant them in midsummer and overwinter to harvest in early spring the following year. These need the harsh conditions of cold northern winters to do well.

In all cases, give the plants a site out of the wind, where there is plenty of sun and space them about 50-75 cm/1½-2½ ft apart all round.

Legumes

One of my favourite beans is the broad bean; eaten raw with a piece of cheese, the young beans are a delicious and far more nutritious alternative to biscuits. Broad beans can be sown outdoors from late winter to mid spring in deeply dug soil with plenty of added manure or compost. The seed is large, so it can be station sown in holes made with a dibber, or else be sown in drills; the spacing is about 25 cm/10 in all round and the seed should be set about 2.5 cm/1 in deep. 'Aquadulce' is an exceptionally hardy variety, and can be sown in late autumn to overwinter, the young pods being gathered in spring. The century-old variety 'Bunyards Exhibition' has long pods, while 'Green Windsor', another old stager, has short pods and the beans have a sweeter flavour.

ABOVE: French beans require deep, well-drained soil.

RIGHT: Runner beans have attractive flowers to brighten up your garden.

The main pest affecting broad beans is black fly, which begin to appear about the time the first bean pods are forming. One day the plants will be clean, the next the growing tips will be coated in a varnish of shiny black insects. The best way to avoid this is to pinch out the succulent growing tips that attract the insects, removing the top 10 cm/4 in of growth. They can be cooked like spinach in a little boiling water, served with butter and salt and pepper, and have the delicious flavour of broad beans.

Support the beans by encircling the row with some garden twine looped around stakes that are spaced 1 m/3 ft apart. The smaller-growing varieties will not need this.

Snow peas, mangetout, call them what you like, are another early cropping member of the legume family, one that is especially worth growing, since the price per pound in the greengrocer is high.

Mangetout is French for 'eat all', and that is just what you do since the sweet pods are harvested while the peas are quite immature. Stir-fry the pods in oil or steam them quickly to serve with butter and seasoning.

Like all beans, snow peas like a well-manured soil with plenty of moisture while they grow. Sow the seed late winter, about 1 cm/½ in deep in drills 15 cm/6 in wide spaced 45 cm/18 in apart. The seed is large enough to sow individually and is sown across the drill about 5 cm/2 in apart all round. Use netting or twiggy brushwood to support the plants as they grow.

Gather the pods when they are only the size of your little finger. Pick regularly to keep the plants producing. They freeze well. And if any pods escape, the peas that develop are just as delicious.

Ordinary peas are either first earlies, second earlies or main crop, and can be sown in a similar fashion to snow peas, but starting in late autumn and carrying through to the middle of the next spring for a succession of cropping. 'Feltham First' is good for autumn sowing; 'Wonder' and 'Little Marvel' are dependable first earlies for early spring sowing, then come 'Greenshaft' and 'Markana'.

Mice are a problem and soaking the seed first in paraffin is said to prevent the newly sown seeds being stolen; pigeons like the young shoots. Pea moth can also ruin a crop, filling the pods and peas with tiny white maggots. Prevention is better than cure, so spray the plants with derris about five to seven days after the plants begin to flower.

French beans can be bush or climbing and in either case produce rounded beans best picked when finger-length. They also like well-manured soil and plenty of water. Sow the seed in pots under glass in mid spring to plant out as soon as all danger of frost is past, or in the open ground when the soil is beginning to warm in late spring. Plants should be about 15 cm/6 in apart in double rows 30 cm/1 ft apart. Alternatively, station sow several seeds at this spacing and thin the weaker plants out as they mature.

I like to grow the yellow-podded varieties such as 'Corona d'Oro' to pickle in a sweet-and-sour brine with plenty of mustard seed; and the purple-podded varieties such as 'Royalty' and 'Purple King' have a far better flavour than the common green sorts. The purple colour fades to

ABOVE: Runner beans can be grown in containers, but must have a support to climb; a simple bamboo cane tepee is a good solution.

dark green on cooking. 'Blue Lake' is a dependable green climbing bean; 'Tendergreen' is stringless. But – if picked young – beans won't be stringy anyway. As with all legumes, it is important to keep picking to keep the plants producing. Aphids can be bothersome, so take the necessary measures with insecticides.

Runner beans are probably the most popular bean for the home gardener, and no wonder when you compare the flavour and snap of a freshly picked runner with the limp impostors from the supermarket shelf. Start runners indoors as you would French beans, or sow the seed outdoors in prepared ground from the end of spring or as soon as the soil begins to warm. Runners are greedy feeders and like deeply dug soil to which plenty of manure or compost has been added the previous autumn. They also require lots of water, and lining the trench with shredded newspaper can help improve moisture retention in the soil. Seed should be set at least 5 cm/2 in deep and about 15 cm/6 in apart.

Runner beans are vigorous climbers, so be sure the supports you provide are substantial, either set in a tepee arrangement of stout canes, or in double rows of poles and canes.

The pests that gardeners growing runner beans will have to guard against include blackfly, pigeons and mice.

The Alliums

Onions like a light, rich, well-drained soil in a sunny, open site. They can be raised in the same location of the vegetable garden every year, so don't have to fit into the overall rotational scheme. But in this case it is especially important to prepare the soil well, digging deep and adding plenty of compost or well-rotted manure. Onions can be raised from seed or from small bulbs or sets. If using seed, sow in shallow drills about 30 cm/12 in apart and thin to between 10-15 cm/4-6 in apart. Follow a similar planting scale for onion sets. One useful fact about onions to bear in mind is that the further apart the seeds or sets are placed, the larger the bulb will grow.

Begin sowing seed or planting sets in early spring, and continue with seed for successive crops until early summer. Japanese onion sets are for overwintering, and if planted in late summer or early autumn will be ready to harvest in the spring. Unlike the ordinary onions, they do not store well and so I like to use them fresh from the ground, pulling them as they are needed.

'Red Brunswick' is a lovely grapey-red onion that looks good in salads, while 'Sturon' makes a good, golden, globe-shaped onion; 'Stuttgart Giant' makes a flat-bottomed bulb. Onions grown from seed are more susceptible to attack from onion fly.

By midsummer, the green tops of the onions will begin to wither; fold the stalks over close to the bulb so that the onion is exposed to the ripening effects of the sun. After a week or so of warm weather the onions will be ready to lift. Do this by

BELOW: These onions are being planted as sets. They will ripen more quickly than onions grown from seed, and are more resistant to pests and fungi.

gently raising each onion from the ground with a garden fork. Turn the onion up so the roots can dry in the sun. Gather them in and either make plaits (braids) of the dried leaves or trim the bulbs neatly and store in a net bag. A cool, dry place is best for storing onions.

Shallots have a milder flavour than onions. They are usually grown from sets, spaced as for onions, planted in early spring; or, if overwintering types are used, in the middle of autumn for harvesting in early summer. One set will produce a cluster of bulbs. 'Dutch Yellow' is a popular variety.

Garlic is good for your health, so grow plenty of it and use it whenever you can. Plant individual segments (a garlic bulb is made of many separate cloves) in late summer in rich soil. They take a long time to develop, and will be ready to lift the following summer.

When planting sets and cloves, don't be tempted to screw the little bulbs into the ground; you'll damage the end that needs to take root. Take a shallow drill and line out the sets, then draw the soil over them and firm the bulbs into the ground with the back of your rake, or by treading around them carefully. There should be a tuft of the papery topknot of each set showing above the ground. Birds see these as a tempting treat,

BELOW: Once harvested, keep onions hung up in a cool place, where they can stay dry until they are ready to be eaten.

ABOVE: Plant garlic in late summer and leave it to overwinter. It will be ready to lift early the next summer.

ABOVE: Rhubarb can be cultivated with little effort.

and they will pull the sets out. Black thread or humming tape suspended above the rows should keep birds away. Rake Bromophos into the soil before planting to prevent infestation by onion fly.

Vegetable Fruits

Unless you are mad about it, one or two plants will keep the average family in enough rhubarb to eat fresh, bottle or freeze. Give it a corner of the vegetable garden where it can be heaped with manure to feed it, covered with a bucket to blanch the young stalks in early spring, and generally be out of the way of the day-to-day running of the garden.

Rhubarb plants are usually bought as crowns – although it is perfectly easy to raise from seed – but with a crown you are more certain to have a good variety. Plant the crowns so that the buds are just above the level of the soil and space them about 1m/3 ft apart. Water in well and top-dress with compost or well-rotted manure each spring.

Courgettes and marrows also like a good deal of manure or compost, so prepare a planting site by digging a generously-sized hole and filling it with either material. Sow the seeds in individual pots (two or three to a pot to thin later to the strongest plant) in early to mid spring to plant out as soon as all danger of frost has passed. Alternatively, you can sow the seed *in situ*. Give the plants plenty of water, and keep picking. Courgettes should be harvested when they are about 10 cm/4 in long, or as soon as

LEFT: The marrow, like the cauliflower, is a vegetable that often features in garden-show competitions. It is worth bearing in mind that the larger the fruit, the higher the water content, and the less flavour it will have.

the flower on the tip of the developing fruit withers. It is astonishing how quickly a courgette can turn into a fruit the size of a rugby ball. Marrows are raised in the same fashion, but since the aim is to have large fruit, they should be fed and watered routinely.

If the leaves show signs of yellow spotting and withering, you are faced with an outbreak of the mosaic virus, for which there is no cure except to dig up the plants and burn them.

Asparagus is usually grown from crowns purchased as named varieties; 'Lucullus' is a good one to look for, since it is an all-male variety – this means you won't have to worry about removing seed-bearing fronds from female plants, which would be weakened if left to reproduce.

Plant the crowns in the spring in a prepared bed. This will be the permanent home for the crop, so take time to do the job well the previous autumn, making sure to remove any perennial weed roots and digging in plenty of compost and manure.

It will be at least two to three years before the crops are really worthwhile, and the first few years while the bed is becoming established require patience; you must not cut any in the year after planting, and then cut only one or two spears from each crown in the second year. After that, cut the largest spears first, making the cut just under the soil surface.

After the harvest in early summer, allow the plants to develop the feather fronds of foliage, which are an attractive addition to the garden. Cut these down at the end of summer, remove any weeds and give the bed a good blanket of compost or rotted manure.

It is only necessary to prepare a raised bed on which to grow asparagus if the soil is very heavy. In this case you must double dig, adding rubble to the bottom of the trench to improve the drainage before back filling with compost and topsoil.

Slugs and snails will feed on shoots as they emerge, causing damage, while asparagus beetle – distinguished by the bright orange markings on its black body – goes for the stems and foliage. You can control the beetle with the application of derris powder.

RIGHT: Supermarket courgettes are green, but the gardener can raise different varieties – such as these yellow ones.

THE FRUIT GARDEN

While the commercial grower must concentrate on producing fruit in quantity, the home gardener can time their harvest to pick the fruit when it is sweetest and juiciest.

SOFT FRUIT HAS ALWAYS been included in the kitchen garden and in fact makes a most decorative addition. Strawberries can be used to edge the paths through the garden, raspberry canes laden with ripening fruit make an attractive backdrop to rows of lettuces and carrots, while gooseberries can be trained as standards to make topiary-style features.

Within each group there are varieties to choose for early-, mid- or late-season ripening. But plant breeders have been busy with our traditional soft fruits and there are now varieties that bear throughout the seasons (with the exception of winter of course), making these varieties especially suited to small gardens.

Raspberries and Blackberries

These are the best of the summer soft fruit crop, and few things taste as good as a handful of sun-warmed berries fresh from the cane. Birds also like the bright red berries, so – as with most soft fruit – it is advisable to put netting over the canes or devise some other foolproof bird scarer.

Raspberries like cool, moist soil, and can be grown in shady spots in the garden. It takes the canes at least two years to come into full cropping; but once they are established, and if you care for them well, you can continue to gather for at least 10 years. So when choosing the site, be sure it is some place where the canes can be left undisturbed.

ABOVE: The raspberry cane will fruit after two years.

RIGHT: Blackberries should be planted in well-drained soil.

If the site is located in a sunny part of the garden, however, put a thick mulch around the base of plants and water frequently in dry spells. Dig the soil deeply and add plenty of well-rotted manure or compost to aid moisture retention.

Canes are usually best planted in the autumn so that they can put down roots and begin production of new fruiting wood the following season.

There is no need to plant deeply, just be sure the crown is covered by about 5 cm/2 in of topsoil. Tread the soil gently around the roots to firm the plant in the hole and then water well. Cut the canes back to within 30 cm/12 in of the ground. Set the plants about 90 cm/3 ft apart in the row and if you are planting more than one row of raspberries, they should be no less than 1.2m/4 ft apart.

There are several ways to train raspberry canes, but the easiest method – and the one best suited to the small garden – is to tie the canes to parallel wires that have been stretched between two stakes. Keep the row free of weeds so there is no competition for the newly planted canes, and in the first year you can remove the flowers to concentrate the plants' energies on producing the canes.

As new canes appear, tie them loosely to the training wires with soft garden twine. Fruit is produced on the lateral or side growths coming from new canes. Follow a strict pruning regime to clear away the old canes at the end of the cropping season, leaving only six to eight new canes. Be sure the remaining canes are securely fastened to the wires so that winter winds won't rock the plants. In early spring, trim these back to about one-third of their length. Suckers will no doubt begin to appear some distance from the parent plant. These should be pulled from the ground and not dug out with a spade, which would only encourage them to grow more strongly.

ABOVE: Tie canes loosely to the training wire with soft twine.

In early spring and again in autumn give the row a top-dressing of sulphate of potash. When you water, always do so at the base of the plants, never as an overhead shower, and remember that mulching will keep weeds down and help the soil to retain moisture.

'Autumn Bliss' crops from late summer until the first frosts of autumn. 'Glen Prosen' crops in midsummer. 'Allgold', a natural sport of 'Autumn Bliss', has sweet yellow fruit.

Blackberries have been grown in gardens since the earliest times, and although the fruit gathered from the hedgerows is nicely flavoured, garden-cultivated varieties produce better quality berries. It is worth giving space to at least one or two plants. But since blackberries are easy to propagate (a new plant will grow wherever a cane touches the ground) one plant may be all you'll need.

'Himalaya Giant' deserves its name for the robust canes it will produce, making it one for the large garden. 'Oregon Thornless' and 'Loch Ness' (a relatively newer variety) are thornless, and better suited to small gardens – and are far easier to pick!

Loganberries are a cross between blackberries and raspberries, producing large, slightly acid fruit. 'Thornless' is the variety to look for, but it will take plenty of space. It is good for covering fences – train it against wires stretched between the supporting posts. Boysenberry and tayberry are midsummer fruiting hybrids, the product of crosses between various species of *Rubus*, the genus to which these fruits belong.

All the above require similar conditions to raspberries; deeply dug, moist soil with plenty of added manure or compost. Plants are usually purchased in the autumn and should be planted immediately with the crown about 8 cm/3 in below the soil. If you are growing more than one plant, be sure to space them at least 2.5-3m/8-10 ft apart. I have always grown these berries against fences or trelliswork; the long trailing canes can also be trained to grow over ornamental arches in the garden.

After planting, cut the canes down to a bud, about 25 cm/10 in from the base of the plant. Mulch well. As the new canes grow during the first summer, tie them to wires to create a fan-shaped arrangement. New canes will develop the following season; as they do, gather them together in a loose bundle and tie out of the way of the old canes that will be bearing fruit. As cropping comes to an end on these canes, cut them out completely and tie in the new canes in their place.

Keep the plants mulched and water well if conditions are especially dry. In winter, top-dress the soil around the base of the plants with sulphate of potash.

Gooseberries have ranked as Britain's most popular garden fruit since at least the late 13th century. By the

18th century there were nearly 300 named varieties in cultivation. Goosberries like a light soil that is slightly acid, and well-drained soil to which plenty of manure or compost has been added. But, since gooseberries make their roots very near the surface, moisture is important – mulch well to conserve water in the soil. There is a disease specific to this fruit, American gooseberry mildew, so avoid high-nitrogen fertilisers that would encourage too much leafy growth.

Gooseberry bushes are extremely prickly and it can be quite a chore to harvest the berries; for this reason it is a good idea to plant the bushes in cordons, pruning and training them to grow in an upright manner. This also makes it easier to grow gooseberries in a small garden or in containers.

To start a cordon, begin with a young bush that has a single strong-growing, upright main branch; this is the leader. Plant out in a well-prepared site; planting distance for cordons is between 40-50 cm/15-20 in apart. Cut the growing tip back by about half its length as measured from the topmost side shoot or lateral, making the cut just above a bud. Cut away any branches growing below 10 cm/4 in of the ground, and trim back all the laterals to 2.5 cm/1 in from the main stem, making the cut just above an upwards-facing bud.

The next summer, cut the new growth on the laterals back to about 10 cm/4 in. The bud at the top of the leader will have grown; do not prune this but tie it loosely to the support.

Repeat the winter and summer pruning until the cordon has reached the desired height; the optimum is about 1.5m/5 ft. Leveller is probably the most popular variety, producing good crops of large yellow berries that can be cooked or eaten as a dessert fruit when fully ripened.

ABOVE: **This gooseberry bush has been grown as a standard; the plant has been trained to grow in an upright manner, making the fruit easy to pick.**

ABOVE: **Pruning white currants so that the fruit spurs have a lot of space around them will ensure top-quality fruit for your desserts.**

RIGHT: The 'Whinham's Industry' gooseberry produces a ruby-red fruit that is ready to pick in mid season. But the plant is prone to mildew.

BELOW: Late-flowering 'Malling Jet' blackcurrants are less susceptible to frosts.

ABOVE: Prune blackcurrant bushes in winter, cutting back all the branches on an old woody bush like this except for the six strongest growths.

Blackcurrants, redcurrants and white currants are near relatives of the gooseberry and even greedier feeders, with the blackcurrant the hungriest of them all. When preparing the planting site, it is just as well to dig in as much manure or compost as is possible, to give the bushes the best start in life you can.

Planting should be done in mid autumn, allowing about 1.5m/5 ft between each bush. Blackcurrant bushes should be planted slightly deeper than they were in the container or nursery bed. Redcurrants and white currants, however, are grown on a single stem to form a small trunk supporting a head with many branches.

Pruning a blackcurrant bush begins as soon as it is planted by cutting back all the shoots to within 5 cm/2 in of the ground. Make the cuts above outward-facing buds, so the branch that develops from the the bud will be growing outwards and upwards, not inwards or sideways. Blackcurrants fruit on the previous season's wood, and pruning is done in the winter. The aim is to clear out dead wood or weak growths, cutting these shoots out completely. Then cut away any old wood that has not developed new side growths. Where old wood has developed side shoots, cut it back to a healthy new growth.

Leave any new wood that has grown from the base of the plant. Gooseberry bushes are pruned in the same manner.

Redcurrants and white currants are pruned to achieve an open crown on top of a single stem or trunk. This is done by a routine of winter and summer pruning. Begin in the winter after planting by pruning out all but the strongest-growing side growths; these will form the main branches. Cut back hard all side growths developing along these branches, and cut the growing tips or leaders back by about a third each season. In several years you should have a bush with about six to eight main branches.

In winter, cut these back to an outward facing bud. In summer, cut back the side shoots developing along the branches to about five leaves from the base of the shoot.

Like gooseberries, currants and other shallow rooters also benefit from a moisture-conserving mulch, which has the added advantage of helping keep weeds down; this is important because berries dislike competition from other plants, and react badly to having their roots disturbed by the hoeing necessary when digging up weeds.

Whichever variety you choose, be it the red-fruiting 'Laxton's No 1', 'White Versailles' or, with its large clusters of black berries, 'Boskoop Giant', always be sure to obtain stock that is certified as virus free.

Use derris to control attacks of sawfly caterpillars which can defoliate gooseberry and blackcurrant bushes in what seems minutes. Gall mite, also known as big bud mite, attacks currants, favouring especially black-

ABOVE: Fruit cages will protect bushes from birds.

RIGHT: Redcurrants are ready for harvesting from midsummer on.

ABOVE: Gall mite has infested the stem on the right.

currants . They are responsible for spreading reversion virus (from which nursery stock should be certified as being free). In this case prevention is much better than cure, and a routine spring spray of lime sulphur or other proprietary deterrent should be applied.

ABOVE: Strawberries are relatively easy to look after, and don't take up a great deal of room in the garden.

If you grow only one fruit, you ought to make it strawberries; even a few plants should provide you with a bowlful or two of sweet berries. If you grow the wild or alpine sorts, you can use them as edging around flowerbeds, and dot the perpetual fruiting sorts such as 'Aromel' among the flowers. Otherwise, the early fruiting 'Elvira' and the later 'Cambridge Favourite' are reliable for a succession crop. However, I find 'Aromel' produces heavy crops for two years, then I have to renew the rows from the plants produced on the trailing runners. Since these appear every year, it is easy to establish consecutive rows for peak performance.

ABOVE: These strawberries are afflicted with grey mould, a danger in humid weather.

Strawberries love sunshine and a moisture-retentive, light soil that has been well-manured. Set the plants in rows about 60 cm/2 ft apart, with about 45 cm/18 in between each one. Mulch between the rows with a layer of clean straw. This will keep

ABOVE: The netting placed over these strawberries should keep birds away, but keep a watch for any holes in the netting – any birds that get under the net could become trapped.

the fruit clean (washing soil off strawberries spoils the flavour of the fruit), and helps to maintain the roots in cool and moist conditions. During the first season after planting, remove all the flowers so that the plant's energy goes into producing strong roots rather than fruit. After that, you can allow them to flower and fruit.

As runners are produced, they can be pegged down in position to make new rows either side of the mother plant. Only permit as many runners as you need plants to develop; remove all the others. When they have developed good roots, lift them to establish neat rows if necessary. Treat them as you would new plants, removing flowers and so on.

Feed plants with a late winter dressing of sulphate of potash, but avoid high nitrogen fertilisers, which would only promote leaf growth. Water during warm weather as the first fruit begins to set, and stop watering as it begins to ripen.

Birds love strawberries, so netting is essential. You can make elaborate cages to enclose completely the soft fruit garden, but I find that a length of garden netting stretched loosely over the fruit keeps off all but the most persistent birds. Use slug bait to keep that pest at bay. In warm, humid weather, grey mould can be a problem, and the best way to avoid that is not to plant too closely and keep weeds down so that air can circulate freely between the plants.

Tree Fruit

Fruit trees make a beautiful contribution to the garden. In my garden one of the joys of spring is the small orchard of a dozen old varieties of apple laden with bloom and the promise of a golden harvest in late summer. Bees buzz through the boughs. The scent, for apple blossom does have fragrance, is as sweet and delicate as the blush rose tint of the petals. Few of our apples make it to storage, since eating them straight from the tree as they ripen is my reward for pruning, spraying and winter washing the trees to ensure unblemished fruit. In the garden there are also espalier pear trees against warm walls, a greengage plum, two quince trees, a mulberry and a medlar. I choose fruit varieties just as I do vegetables – on the principle of growing what I can not readily obtain in the market.

My neighbour does the opposite and grows things more commonly found in the supermarket: he has filled his garden with fruit trees. There are a dozen 'Cox' and 'Bramley' apple trees and half-a-dozen 'Victoria' and 'Czar' plum trees. The plums perform with gusto (which is why I haven't bothered to plant my own purple plums – my neighbour is a generous friend), but others might find 'Cox' and 'Bramley' apples better suited to commercial orchards and that style of management, than to the domestic garden.

Our trees are grown on dwarfing stock, which makes trees a manageable size. There is a super-dwarfing stock producing trees that are suitable for container growing. Most fruit trees are grafted to control their growth, provide vigour and so on, and also to provide enough trees to satisfy the demands of garden centres. When purchasing trees, do so from a reputable, specialist nurseryman who will be able to provide you with healthy trees and detailed advice to ensure you get the best tree for your garden.

Generally, most trees like an open, sunny spot, but with some shelter from strong winds. If you look at a commercial orchard, you will notice that a shelter belt of conifers or other fast-growing tree has been planted to screen the orchard from the prevailing winds.

While fruit trees can be grown on just about any kind of soil, they will only do well where there is a good depth of topsoil on a free-draining site. Simply digging a hole in your garden will tell you what the conditions are; make the test hole at least 1m/3 ft deep, and lay each spadeful of soil separately on the ground as it is removed. By examining the excavations and the removed soil, you can establish the depth of the topsoil, whether it is clay, loam, sand or a variously proportioned mixture of these types, and what the state of the subsoil is; clay, rock, gravel, and so on.

ABOVE: A well-tended plum tree, such as this Mirabelle de Nancy, will produce a bountiful harvest each year.

RIGHT: This apple tree has been espaliered – trained to grow against horizontal wire supports.

Now you must fill the hole with water. How quickly does it drain away? If it sits there for a few hours, you will have to break up the bottom of each planting hole you dig and incorporate gravel and small pieces of broken rubble to improve the drainage at the bottom of the hole as well as into the backfill (the soil removed from the hole).

But if the water drains away immediately, it will help to dig in as much well-rotted manure or compost as you can. This humus greatly improves the moisture-retaining quality of loose, sandy soils. Otherwise, the fruit tree's roots might never get enough water for decent growth.

Like vegetables and soft fruits, fruit trees have their preferences too. Plums can be grown on the heaviest clay soils, and are the least fussy fruit about drainage. Pears can also settle into a heavy soil – as long as it is well-drained. Cooking apples can cope with a heavy soil, but only if you have improved it and ensured that the drainage is good. By contrast, dessert varieties are much more temperamental, and need the best conditions you can provide – well-drained land, with a deep layer of topsoil – to do well. Cherries are surface rooters, and prefer deep, loamy topsoils over chalk or gravel to provide the best drainage.

ABOVE: A 'Morello' cherry

BELOW: Plum in blossom

Perfect Planting

The best time to plant is during the autumn, whether the tree is purchased as a container-grown plant from a garden centre or a bare root from a specialist nursery. Then there will be less need to water since autumn rains will help keep the soil moist, and the tree will be dormant; instead of striving to make top growth and new roots, it can concentrate its energies on settling into its new home.

If the trees have been purchased with bare roots, and arrive late in the season when there may be hard frosts or other adverse weather conditions preventing you from planting, it is essential to heel in the roots by covering the root ball with soil or moist peat. Lay the tree on a shallow angle in a trench and heap soil over the roots, then cover the top with sacking or horticultural fleece just to protect the tips from freezing dessication.

Wait for a still, bright day to do the planting. Dig a hole that is at least twice as large as the circumference of the root ball and deep enough to accommodate the roots but, and this is critical, the tree must not be planted any deeper than it was in its container or in the nursery bed. This last depth can be recognised by a difference in colour at the base of the stem; the below-soil level area will be darker.

Don't scatter the backfill all around, but place it in a single heap by the side of the hole. Do what is necessary to improve the hole's drainage and soil condition as described on the previous page. If no improvement is necessary, use the garden fork to prick holes into the base and sides.

Examine the root ball of the tree. If there are any damaged or withered roots, cut them away. Now check the depth of the hole by standing the tree in it and laying a spade across the top of the hole; is the nursery line level with the handle of the spade?

If it is, the hole is the correct depth. Otherwise, make the necessary adjustments.

Begin to backfill by throwing a few spadefuls of soil over the roots. Work the soil between them by shaking the tree gently up and down. Put back just enough soil to hold the tree upright. Then hammer in the stake.

Trees need to be staked to hold them upright while they establish roots. Without stakes, wind and weather would jostle them about, blow them over and otherwise prevent them from becoming established. Stakes can be purchased from a garden centre. They should be at least 75 cm/2 ft deep, long enough to be buried with 45-75 cm/18-24 in above ground to which the tree is secured by tree ties. It really won't do to use bits of old plumbing, sticks foraged from the hedges, bits of plastic baling twine and old pantyhose. You'll have paid enough to obtain a good tree, so do the same for the stake and tie. They will remain in place for at least three years, as a feature of your garden.

ABOVE: The arch in this garden has been created by training two apple trees to grow across the path.

Pound the stake into the bottom of the hole, avoiding the tree roots and taking care to see that it is vertical and about 5 cm/2 in from the tree. Position the stake on the side of the prevailing wind, so that in a strong wind the tree will strain away from the stake and away from any possible damage. Secure the tree temporarily to the stake with a tie, and then complete the backfilling. Add a few handfuls of bone meal to the soil as you spade it into the hole and, when the job is nearly complete, gently tread the soil in around the base of the tree.

When all the soil has been returned, tighten the tie permanently (if you can't work out how the buckle operates, have it demonstrated to you at the garden centre. It should end with a loop around the tree and a loop around the stake). Traditionally stakes were much longer, but I prefer the

ABOVE: **In this geometrically laid out garden, apple trees stand guard over the strawberry plants beneath.**

RIGHT: **If your garden has a light, well-drained soil, you might find a walnut tree will make a handsome addition.**

LEFT: The apple tree's blossoms have a subtle fragrance to match their delicate colour.

RIGHT: The pears harvested from your gaden will be markedly superior in taste and texture to commercially grown varieties.

shorter length as it permits the tree some movement of the developing trunk which helps it to grow more quickly into a stout support.

Apply a blanket of mulch around the base of the tree to keep down weeds and grass and to conserve moisture as the seasons progress. Pay particular attention to weeds during the spring when all plants are making the most growth, including the fruit trees. As root systems establish, they do not need competition for the available moisture and nutrients. This is less important in the summer when the tree will be able to draw on its reserves of moisture and food collected during the spring and stored in the wood. In fact, a bit of leanness now will help the fruit to mature and the new wood to ripen.

BELOW: If you plant a chestnut tree make sure it's a sweet chestnut if you're after good eating. The horse chestnut is for good conkers!

Harvesting and Storing

When fruit begins to ripen, it is beginning the downward journey to decay; when harvesting for storage, you must try to judge the moment when the fruit is no longer immature, but has not yet fully ripened. A ripe fruit will not only soon lose its flavour, it will also not store well.

Generally, the moment can be judged by eye – when the flush of ripeness tints the skin – and touch. The fruit should lift off the tree: that moment when it doesn't have to be pulled off, which would damage the fruit and the tree, nor does it fall instantly into your hand. Taking the fruit in your cupped hand and gently lifting upwards, the

fruit comes cleanly away with stem attached. This is important, as stemless fruit will not keep well.

Take care when harvesting not to damage the unblemished fruit you have worked hard to produce. Lay it gently in a basket or box; any bruising, which in the case of such soft fruits as peaches, nectarines and apricots can happen with the slightest squeeze, will give an opening to rot.

Don't harvest all in one day, do it gradually because the fruit won't all be ripening at the same rate. Take every fruit from the tree, good, bad and indifferent.

Of course there are some fruits which are purposefully picked when green – gooseberries, pears and plums for bottling; cooking apples for baking. These you gather as you need. Some of the late maturing varieties also should be gathered carefully and allowed to ripen in store.

You may have seen pictures of the amazing fruit stores in Victorian kitchen gardens; rows of open-slatted shelves that pulled out of the supporting frame on silent runners. The purpose was to keep the fruit separate in airy conditions in a cool dark place. The store had to have a degree of ambient humidity, since in dry conditions the fruit would shrivel, while too much moisture would make it rot.

In modern gardens space may be limited, but a shelving stack in the shed or garage should provide enough space to keep at least some of the harvest. I use the plastic boxes in which mushrooms are delivered to supermarkets; they have perforated sides and bottoms and are formed to stack without interfering with the contents of the box below. You can take the trouble to wrap each fruit in a twist of paper, but generally the less handling the better.

Failing the space (or the inclination) to store fresh fruit, there is always bottling and freezing – any good cookery book would provide you with instructions on how to proceed.

ABOVE: These apples have been stored in sawdust, which will help keep them dry.

RIGHT: This apple tree is ready for another good harvest, but even without the fruit you'll find they make attractive trees worthy of any garden.

The Fruit

APPLES

Apples are usually grafted on rootstocks, each with a different quality. In Britain, for example, the rootstock is identified by a number prefixed with M, referring to the East Malling Research Station in Kent, where much work was done on developing apple varieties for commercial orchards and domestic gardens. M27 is the smallest one, making trees suitable for container growing, while M9 is a commonly encountered stock, producing compact trees suitable for small orchards; trees for espalier, fan and special training are often grown on this stock. Discuss your requirements with the nurseryman to be sure you obtain the tree best suited to your needs.

ABOVE: The 'Spartan' apple is a late-season ripener. The tree will give you a heavy crop.

LEFT: Crab apple trees are colourful both in spring and in the autumn.

ABOVE: Scab is just one of the numerous diseases to which apples are prone. They also suffer from a wide range of pests, such as woolly aphids and codling moth.

Many apple varieties have to be pollinated by another apple of a different variety to produce fruit; this means they must each flower at the same time. Just to confuse matters, some, such as the 'Blenheim Orange' or the 'Bramley's Seedling', require two different pollinators. Again, seek the advice of the nurseryman, or you may end up with nothing but a lovely show of apple blossom!

In a small garden, one of the best ways to grow fruit is as a cordon against a fence along which heavy galvinised wire has been stretched. You should find three parallel wires about 1m/3 ft apart is enough. Next, attach a bamboo cane about 2m/6 ft long at right angles to the wires. The cordon is trained to this, and gradually lowered to a 45-degree angle.

Plant the trees in the autumn about 1m/3 ft apart. Cut back any side shoots that are longer than 10 cm/4 in to three buds from the base of the shoot where it meets the main stem. Take care not to damage the growing tip of the main stem. Remove all the blossom in the first year.

The first summer after planting, with the main stem still attached to the cane, cut back all the mature side shoots (laterals) growing from the main stem to three leaves above the basal cluster (the group of leaves you'll find growing where the side shoot meets the main stem). If any side shoots are growing off these laterals, prune them back to one leaf.

Repeat this pruning sequence each summer. Begin to lower the apple into position by shifting the cane into an angle, about 5 degrees each year.

Not all the flowers will develop into fruit; there will be some natural wastage as immature fruit drop from the developing cluster. But you must also help by thinning out the clusters to remove any diseased or damaged fruit, leaving one or two fruits on each.

'Blenheim Orange' is a good dual-purpose apple; 'Egremont Russet' has a fine almond-like flavour, while 'Pitmaston Pineapple' has a hint of honey; 'Lord Lambourne' will give you heavy crops of crisp, juicy apples.

Codling moth and canker do the most damage to apple trees. The first can be controlled by tying grease bands around the trunk of the tree in late spring to trap grubs and spray trees with a spring wash or multi-purpose insecticide/fungicide. Other pests such as bud moth, winter moth, and woolly aphid can be controlled with a tar-oil wash in winter. The only remedy for canker is to prune off diseased wood or else pare away the diseased portion. Burn all diseased prunings. Several varieties, including 'Cox's Orange Pippin', are especially prone to canker; check with the nurseryman before purchasing; if you are only going to grow a few apples, why give space to a poor performer?

PLUMS AND GAGES

Trees bearing plums and gages tend to be quite large, so two or three mature ones will provide you with plenty of fruit both to eat fresh and to preserve. The most popular varieties of plum are 'Czar' and 'Victoria'; the former makes heavy crops of small inky-purple fruit good for cooking or eating fresh when ripe, and the later makes rosy-purple oval fruit with a mild flavour, best eaten fresh. 'Golden Transparent' and 'Oullin's Gage' are particularly succulent and aromatic gages. It's a yearly contest between me and the wasps to see who gets to them first!

Before planting the trees in well-cultivated soil, add a dressing of lime, unless your soil is already quite alkaline. Once the tree is established, pruning begins by reducing laterals that are crowded or crossing each other to within four or five buds of their base; leave all the open, robust laterals unpruned. Leaders should be pruned back by about one-third of their length each year in order to establish a strong framework. Once this is achieved, just keep the tree tidy by removing dead and weak wood and shortening the crossing laterals as they appear.

Pruning should be done during the growing season and all wounds should painted immediately with a proprietary wound paint for fruit trees.

Leaf curl is carried by aphids, causing the leaves to crumple up and developing fruit to drop; it and other pests are controlled by winter tar-oil wash. Silver leaf curl is a devastating fungoid disease recognised by the marked silvering of the leaves and withering of branches which show a brown stain when split. Cut away all the diseased and dead wood and burn; badly infected trees should be destroyed.

ABOVE: These plums have been attacked by brown rot, a fungoid disease that is difficult to control.

PEARS

Pears only really perform well in warm southern regions, finding the rigours of short northern seasons not to their liking. But given protection for the blossom in the early spring and the shelter of a warm, south-facing spot, some pears will provide a harvest of juicy ivory-fleshed fruit. 'Olivier des Serres' and 'Beurre Dumont' are especially succulent late-ripening pears; 'William's Bon Chretien' and 'Conference' are widely popular.

Pear trees respond well to cordon training; the methods you use are similar to that applied to apple trees.

After planting, prune side shoots longer than 10 cm/4 in to three leaves. Attach the leader to the cane and wires. Each summer cut back side shoots longer than 20 cm/8 in to three leaves above the basal cluster. When the leader has reached the desired length, cut it back the new growth at the tip to 12 mm/½ in each summer. Pears require a pollinator so be sure to plant at least two varieties that flower at the same time. Ask the nurseryman for guidance.

Early spring washes should take care of insects such as pear midge and blister mite. The fungus disease pear scab, when

BELOW: A blood, fish and bone meal fertiliser is applied to pear cordons.

ABOVE: Pear trees can be grown in cordons like apple trees. Here a side stem is being pruned back.

ABOVE: The 'Morello' cherry is self-fertile, although you will get a better crop if you have another variety in the garden that flowers at the same time, such as 'Bradbourne Black'.

the fruit discolours and develops deep cracks, can be prevented by spraying with an appropriate fungicide as soon as the blossoms open and again as the flowering finishes.

CHERRIES

Birds provide pretty stiff competition for the ripening cherry crop, so it is best to grow them as fans against a warm wall. This makes it easier to net the tree. Cherries like a light loamy soil that is fairly alkaline and well-drained.

Begin the fan by choosing a maiden tree that has plenty of healthy laterals from which to select four to make the first ribs of the fan. They should be between 30-45 cm/12-18 in from the ground.

Cherries are pruned during the spring and summer to reduce the risk of canker; it also reduces the amount of leafy growth, thus encouraging fruit buds to form at the base of the previous season's laterals. In the first spring after planting cut back the main stem as far as the topmost of the four selected laterals. Cut back the selected laterals to 45-60 cm/18-24 in, making the cut above an upward facing bud. Remove all the other lateral branches. Tie in the first ribs to wires trained against a wall against a wall at 15 cm/6 in intervals.

During the summer, select three strong shoots coming from the pruned laterals; the topmost one will be the main leader of the rib, the remaining two, one on top and below, will be allowed to grow on. Tie these into the wire as they grow. Remove all the other shoots. Repeat this process each year until the fan is well filled with evenly spaced branches coming from the main ribs.

The varieties 'Early Rivers' and 'Morello' are popular, but as with most fruit it is necessary to grow more than one variety for pollination; even though some cherries are self-fertile they will crop better if another variety is planted nearby.

Cherry blackfly is the worst pest and stems and leaves can be coated in a mass of the glossy black insects; be vigilant during the spring and spray with an insecticide at the first sight of the fly. Other insects can be controlled by a regular winter tar-oil wash.

Silver leaf and canker are a fungal threat, treat the former as described in the section on plums and gages, and the latter as described on page 59.

PEACHES, NECTARINES AND APRICOTS

The prima donnas of the fruit garden are peaches, nectarines and apricots. They require more attention than other fruits because of their susceptibility to frost, which will destroy the early appearing flowers. In Victorian kitchen gardens, these fruits were normally grown under glass and were the domain of the head gardener who was responsible for pollinating the flowers, keeping the trees neatly trained and seeing that the fruit reached the table unblemished and at the peak of its perfection.

Apricots are self-fertile, but peaches and nectarines need pollinating by hand. Traditionally this was done with a rabbit's foot kept specially for the job. In many areas, to grow well outdoors they must be trained against a sunny, south-facing wall, usually as a fan. If frost threatens in spring as the flowers form, they must be protected with floating fleece or some other light screen. Plant in rich, deeply dug soil. Plant and fan-train as for cherries. Tar-oil washes in winter and spring sprays with fungicides and insecticides will keep aphids, peach scale and leaf curl under control.

FIGS, FILBERTS AND VINES

Unless you have a really large garden I would not advise attempting to grow your own nuts and figs, although hazel trees and fig trees are highly ornamental. One of the joys of early spring are the dangling golden tassels of a hazel walk underplanted with daffodils. The scent of sun-warmed fig leaves is a garden feature people either love or hate; the huge leathery leaves are deeply lobed and recall to me the sun-drenched gardens of Tuscany. For that reason alone, I grow one against a south-facing wall. It has reached gargantuan proportions, even though the roots are constrained as they should be by stiff clay and concrete pavers lining the sides of hole in which it is planted. These measures are meant to restrict the growth to the benefit of the fruit crop. I do get plenty of fruit on the trees in my garden, but it never ripens. I can only think that there are not enough hot summer days in East Anglia.

Vine fruit such as kiwi are also ornamental, although rather rampageous, which is a drawback since to have fruit on kiwis you need a male and female plant. But a grapevine may give you more pleasure since it is possible to achieve a decent crop from a plant grown as a decorative feature over pergolas and arches.

Grapes will grow in any good soil, preferring an open site with plenty of sun. Plant the vine in early autumn in soil enriched with well-rotted manure. Cut the cane down to leave two or three healthy buds. These will form the rods that are trained up the trellis work or wire supports stretched over the pergola.

In the spring after planting, train the healthiest shoot up the wire; this will be the leader. From it will grow the rods. Tie these into the support to make an evenly spaced network of stems. When this is established, begin a regular system of pruning. Each autumn cut side-shoots emanating from the rods to two buds; these will be the fruiting spurs. Reduce the length of new growth on the rods by half their length. In the spring, pinch out all but the the strongest two shoots growing from the spurs. When these reach 10 cm/4 in, remove the weakest and train in the remaining canes as they grow. When they reach 45 cm/18 in, pinch out the growing tip. Remove all flowers during the first two years.

When the vine is established, each winter reduce the new growth on the rods by half, and cut side shoots back to two buds. In the spring allow the strongest shoot coming from these spurs to grow on, tie it in and eventually pinch out the growing tip after it has made two or three bunches of fruit.

Spray in the spring with a fungicide to avoid mildew.

ABOVE: This peach tree has been fan-trained against the fence behind it.

RIGHT: A grapevine can be a decorative feature, but needs plenty of sun.

ABOVE: In cooler climates, figs are unlikely to ripen to maturity unless they get a lot of hot weather.

INDEX

Canes, 25, 33, 38, 40, 41, 59, 60, 62.
Cloches, 13, 22, 25.
Compost, 8, 10, 11, 12, 16, 24, 28, 30, 33, 35, 36, 38, 41, 42, 43, 50.
Cordons, 42, 59, 60.

Derris, 20, 32, 36, 44.
Diseases: American gooseberry mildew, 42; canker, 25, 59, 61; club root, 21; grey mould, 47; leaf curl, 60, 62; mildew, 62; mosaic virus, 36; peach scale, 62; pear scab, 60; potato blight, 27; silver leaf curl, 60, 61; viruses, 21, 46.
Double digging, 12, 36.

Fertiliser, 12, 14, 22, 24, 27, 28, 29, 30, 32, 33, 35, 36, 38, 41, 42, 43, 46, 47, 50, 52, 62.
Fruits: apples, 50, 56, 59; apricots, 61; asparagus, 36; blackberries, 40; blackcurrants, 43-46; boysenberry, 41; cherries, 50, 61; figs, 62; gages, 60; gooseberries, 38, 41-42, 44, 56; loganberries, 41; marrows, 35; nectarines, 61; peaches, 61; pears, 50, 56, 60; plums, 50, 56, 60; redcurrants, 43-44; rhubarb, 35; storing of, 56; strawberries, 46; tayberry, 41; tomatoes, 12, 16, 21, 24-25; vine fruit, 62; white currants, 43-44.
Fungicide, 16, 21, 27, 62.

Garden lime, 14, 28, 30, 46, 60.
Garden plot: clearing for planting, 12, 33; digging over, 12; location of, 8, 24, 30, 33, 38, 46, 48; plan, 14.
Greenhouses, 13, 16, 61.

Insecticides, 20, 31, 59, 60, 61.

Manure, *see* fertiliser.
Mulch, 10, 24, 40, 41, 42, 44.

Overwintering, 22, 30, 32, 33.

Pests: aphids, 20, 33, 62; asparagus beetle, 36; big bud mite, 44; birds, 34, 38, 47, 61; black fly, 30; blister mite, 60; bud moth, 59; cabbage-root fly, 20; carrot fly, 20, 26; caterpillars, 20, 44; cherry black fly, 61; codling moth, 59; eelworm, 27; flea beetle, 20, 24; gall mite, 44; mice, 32; onion fly, 33, 35; pea moth, 32; pear midge, 60; pigeons, 32; sawfly caterpillars, 44; slugs, 21, 36; winter moth, 59; woolly aphid, 59.
Pricking out, 13, 16.

Pruning: fruit bushes, 40, 42, 43, 44; fruit trees, 59, 60, 61, 62.

Seedbeds, 18, 24, 30, 36.
Seedlings: handling of, 16; vegetable, 16.
Soil: acidity of, 42; alkalinity of, 60, 61; drainage of, 50; quality of, 14, 26, 28, 48, 61.
Sowing, 13, 26, 28, 29; weather for, 13.

Thinning, 18, 26.
Timing: of sowing, 13, 22, 24; of planting, 16, 51; of transplanting, 18, 24; of insecticide spraying, 20, 21; of thinning, 26.
Tools: barrow, 12; garden fork, 51; lawn mower, 11; rake, 13, 28, 34; shredder, 11; spade, 12; trowel, 18.

Vegetables: American cress, 22; beans, 16; beetroot, 26; broad beans, 30, 32; broccoli, 29; Brussels sprouts, 29; cabbage, 18, 28-29; carrots, 25-26, 38; cauliflowers, 30; choosing for garden, 12; corn, 16; courgettes, 12, 35-36; cucumber, 24; French beans, 32-33; garlic, 34; Jerusalem artichoke, 26; leeks, 18; lettuce, 12, 16, 18, 22-25, 38; mangetout, 32; onions, 33-34; parsnips, 25; peas, 16, 32; potatoes, 12, 21, 26; radishes, 24, 25; rocket, 22, 24; runner beans, 33; shallots, 34; spinach, 24; spring onion, 24.

Water and Watering: for sowing, 13, 22; for thinning, 26.
Weeds: removal of, 12.

Picture Acknowledgments

The photographs used in this book have all come from the Garden Picture Library. They are the work of the following photographers:

David Askham: 29, 43(tr); **Jon Bouchier:** 15(b), 17; **Linda Burgess:** 35(t), 38, 46(t); **Brian Carter:** 21(r), 32, 62(t); **Erika Craddock:** 61(b); **John Glover:** 9, 23, 27(t), 35(b), 36, 56, 59(t); **Sunniva Harte:** 18(t); **Marijke Heuff:** 42(t); **Neil Holmes:** 14(tr), 25, 39, 50(b); **Michael Howes:** 12, 13(b), 14(b, tl), 18(b), 19, 20, 21(l), 26(t), 30, 33, 42(b), 43(tl, b), 58, 60(t), 62(b); **Ann Kelley:** 8, 63; **Michele Lamontagne:** 45, 48, 54(t); **Jane Legate:** 44(b), 60(b), 61(t); **Mayer/Le Scanff:** 7, 24, 49, 53, 55, 57; **Jerry Pavia:** 41(b); **Joanne Pavia:** i; **Howard Rice:** 59(b); **Christel Rosenfeld:** 26(b); **J.S. Sira:** 50(t), 54(b); **Ron Sutherland:** 28; **Brigitte Thomas:** 10, 22, 40, 52; **Juliette Wade:** 11, 31, 51; **Mel Watson:** 6, 13(t), 16, 27(b), 37, 41(t), 44(t), 46(b), 47; **Steven Wooster:** ii, 15(t).

The following photographs were taken in the gardens listed:
M van Bennekom's, Netherlands: 42(t); Lackham College Gardens: 29; Littlecote, Berkshire: 21(r); Mien Ruys: ii, 15(t); Preen Manor, Shropshire, England: 9; St Jean de Beauregard, France: 49, 53; Turn End, Buckinghamshire, England: 50(t); Woodpeckers, Warwickshire, England: 31, 51.